Essential COOKING SERIES

COMPREHENSIVE, STEP-BY-STEP COOKING

Soups & Hors D'Oeuvres

HINKLER
BOOKS

HINKLER
BOOKS

Essential Cooking Series: Soups & Hors D'Oeuvres
First published in 2009 by Hinkler Books Pty Ltd
45–55 Fairchild Street
Heatherton Victoria 3202 Australia
www.hinklerbooks.com

Disclaimer: The nutritional information listed under each recipe does not include the nutrient content of garnishes or any accompaniments not listed in specific quantitites in the ingredient list. The nutritional information for each recipe is an estimate only, and may vary depending on the brand of ingredients used, and due to natural biological variations in the composition of natural foods such as meat, fish, fruit and vegetables. The nutritional information was calculated by using Foodworks dietary analysis software (Version 3, Xyris Software Pty Ltd, Highgate Hill, Queensland, Australia) based on the Australian food composition tables and food manufacturers' data. Where not specified, ingredients are always analysed as average or medium, not small or large.

ISBN: 978 1 7418 5706 1

10 9 8 7 6 5 4 3
14 13 12 11 10

Printed and bound in China

Contents

An introduction to soups and hors d'oeuvres

As a savoury entrée or as the centrepiece of a hearty winter's meal, there is nothing as comforting as a bowl of homemade soup. It can be served hot or cold. It can be an elaborate seafood treat brimming with prawns, oysters and fresh herbs or a clever way to resurrect the tired-looking vegetables in the refrigerator crisper. It can be a gourmet adventure introducing the international flavours of a spicy Indian soup or an Italian minestrone. Or it can be a celebration of simple country-style flavours. Soups are an easy, cheap and versatile meal.

Soups are one way to get a dinner party started. Another is to impress your guests with tasty entrées such as Thai fish cakes or potato cakes with smoked salmon. Cold starters like tricolour canapés or sweet capsicum (pepper) terrines can be equally impressive. This book contains an array of soups and other hot and cold starters that will complement any meal.

STOCK

Stocks can either be bought ready-made or made from scratch at home with a minimum of ingredients. If your time is limited there are plenty of good stocks available in supermarkets. Check the labels carefully, however, to avoid soy sauce or other salty flavouring agents.

If you are using a ready-made stock, season your soup only after adding the stock and putting it to the taste test. If you are using powdered stock, keep in mind that they tend to be saltier than liquid stocks.

Freshly made stocks add considerable flavour to soups and if you make them in large batches they can be frozen in airtight containers or in ice-cube trays for later use. With chicken, beef and vegetable stocks, long simmering draws out the flavour of the ingredients, whereas with a fish stock only a little cooking time is required – overcooking can in fact turn the liquid bitter.

The following are recipes for basic stocks:

CHICKEN STOCK

INGREDIENTS

500 g (1 lb) chicken meat and bones
1 onion, chopped
1 carrot, chopped
a handful fresh tarragon, chopped
a handful fresh parsley, chopped
1 bay leaf
salt
1.5 litres (2½ pints) water

1   In a saucepan, place the chicken meat and bones, onion, carrot, herbs and salt. Add hot water just to cover. Bring to a

simmer, reduce heat and simmer gently
for 1 hour. Turn off heat and cool in its
juices. Strain and skim off any fat.

BEEF STOCK
INGREDIENTS

3 litres (5 pints) water
1 kg (2 lb) shin beef bones
360 g (12 oz) gravy beef
2 carrots, unpeeled and cut into chunks
1 large brown unpeeled onion, halved
3 medium pieces unpeeled ginger, sliced
1 cinnamon stick
pinch of salt

6 whole cloves
6 peppercorns
6 coriander (cilantro) seeds
4 whole star anise

1   Place water, shin bones and gravy beef
    in a large pot and bring to the boil,
    skimming off foam with a large metal
    spoon. Reduce heat and simmer, partially
    covered, for 2 hours, skimming often. Add
    remaining stock ingredients and simmer
    for a further 1½ hours. Remove from heat
    and set aside to cool.

2 Drain and reserve stock through a fine sieve and discard bones, carrots, onion and spices. Skim fat from stock.

FISH STOCK

INGREDIENTS

500 g (1 lb) fish pieces and bones
3 sticks celery, roughly chopped
1 carrot, roughly chopped
fresh thyme
1.5 litres (2$\frac{1}{2}$ pints) water

1 Into a saucepan, place the fish bones, celery, carrot, thyme and water. Bring to the boil and simmer for 15–20 minutes. Take care not to overcook. Remove from heat and set aside to cool.

2 Drain and reserve stock through a fine sieve and discard bones, celery, carrot and thyme. Skim fat from stock.

VEGETABLE STOCK

INGREDIENTS

1 tablespoon oil
3 sticks celery, chopped
3 cloves garlic, chopped
1 onion, chopped
1 carrot, chopped
1.5 litres (2$\frac{1}{2}$ pints) water
a handful fresh thyme
1 bay leaf
$\frac{1}{4}$ teaspoon chilli
salt and pepper

1 In a large heavy-based saucepan, heat the oil on a medium heat. Add the celery, garlic, onion and carrot and cook for

5 minutes. Add the water and bring to the boil. Reduce heat and add the thyme, bay leaf, chilli, salt and pepper. Simmer for 1$\frac{1}{2}$–2 hours. Remove from heat and set aside to cool.

2 Drain and reserve stock through a fine sieve and discard celery, carrot, onion and bay leaf.

BLENDING SOUPS

Many of the soups in this book require blending or puréeing after cooking. You can purée soups either in a blender or a food processor. Unless you are using an upright blender, be sure to allow the soup to cool a little before blending or processing. Hot soup in a processor or most blenders could end up all over the kitchen walls and ceiling. The best way to cool soup is to remove it from its cooking pan.

If you are making soups for babies or toddlers, remember to thoroughly check that all the lumps have been removed. Blenders will tend to create a thinner soup than one puréed in a food processor.

STORAGE

Looking for a light lunch or a no-frills Friday evening meal? Easy – defrost and reheat one of the ready-made soups in your freezer. Freezing the leftovers of a huge pot of soup is one of the best things about cooking soups. You can cook as much soup as you like (or your freezer will fit) and none of it needs to be wasted. Most soup will keep in the freezer for 1–3 months or in the refrigerator for up to 3 days.

Roasted capsicum and tomato soup

INGREDIENTS

3 red capsicums (peppers), halved
  and deseeded
1 onion, unpeeled and halved
4 large plum tomatoes
4 cloves garlic, unpeeled
1 $^1/_3$ cups (350 ml, 11 fl oz) chicken or
  vegetable stock
1 tablespoon tomato purée
salt and black pepper
2 tablespoons chopped fresh parsley
serves 4

PREPARATION TIME
15 minutes, plus
10 minutes cooling

COOKING TIME
35 minutes

1 Preheat oven to 200°C (400°F, gas mark 6). Place the capsicums (peppers) and onion on a baking sheet, cut-side down, then add whole tomatoes and garlic. Cook in the oven for 30 minutes or until tender and well browned.

2 Remove from oven and cool for 10 minutes, then peel, discarding skins. Place the vegetables in a food processor with half the stock and process until smooth.

3 Return to the pan, add the remaining stock and tomato purée, stirring to combine, then bring to the boil and cook until heated through. Season to taste and garnish with the parsley just before serving.

NUTRITIONAL VALUE PER SERVE	FAT 0.3 G	CARBOHYDRATE 2.7 G	PROTEIN 1.4 G

Spicy lentil soup

INGREDIENTS

250 g (8 oz) dried split red lentils
1 litre (1²/₃ pints) good-quality
   vegetable stock
1 tablespoon vegetable oil
1 medium onion, finely chopped
1 clove garlic, crushed
2.5 cm (1 in) knob of ginger, finely
   grated
2 teaspoons ground cumin
¹/₂ teaspoon cayenne pepper
salt and black pepper
juice of ¹/₂ lemon
serves 4

1 Place lentils in a sieve and rinse under cold running water, then place in a large pan. Pour over the stock. Bring to the boil, reduce heat, cover and simmer for 20 minutes.

2 Heat oil in a large frying pan, add onion and cook over a gentle heat, stirring occasionally, for 5 minutes or until softened. Add garlic, ginger, cumin and cayenne pepper and cook for a further minute.

3 Add the onion mixture to the lentils, season to taste. Cook for a further 20 minutes, or until lentils are completely soft. Add lemon juice, season to taste and serve.

PREPARATION TIME
10 minutes

COOKING TIME
45 minutes

| NUTRITIONAL VALUE PER SERVE | FAT **1.9** G | CARBOHYDRATE **7.7** G | PROTEIN **5.2** G |

Easy French onion soup

INGREDIENTS

4 tablespoons butter
750 g (1¹/₂ lb) onions, thinly sliced
1 clove garlic, crushed
2 teaspoons plain flour
1.2 litres (2 pints) good-quality
  beef stock
salt and black pepper
4 slices French bread, about
  2.5 cm (1 in) thick
60 g (2 oz) gruyére cheese,
  grated
serves 4

1 Heat the butter in a large heavy-based pan over a low heat until melted and foaming. Add onions and garlic, cover, and cook slowly, stirring often, for 30–35 minutes, until onions are golden brown.

2 Add the flour and cook, stirring constantly, for 2–3 minutes. Gradually pour in the stock, stirring constantly, and bring to the boil. Reduce heat and simmer, covered, for 30 minutes. Season to taste.

3 Preheat grill to high. Toast the French bread on one side, then place grated cheese on uncooked side and grill until melted and browned. Pour soup into warmed serving bowls, placing a piece of cheese toast on each.

PREPARATION TIME
10 minutes

COOKING TIME
1 hour 10 minutes

NUTRITIONAL VALUE PER SERVE   FAT **3.9** G   CARBOHYDRATE **5.1** G   PROTEIN **2.4** G

Provençal-style soup with spring onion pesto

INGREDIENTS

2 tablespoons extra virgin olive oil
1 onion, chopped
1 medium potato, peeled and chopped
1 carrot, chopped
1 yellow capsicum (pepper),
  deseeded and chopped
2 cups (500 ml, 16 fl oz) vegetable stock
2 celery sticks, chopped
2 courgettes (zucchini), chopped
400 g (13 oz) can tomatoes, chopped
1 tablespoon tomato purée
sea salt
freshly ground black pepper
pesto
6 spring onions (green onions),
  chopped with green part
60 g (2 oz) parmesan cheese, grated
4 tablespoons extra virgin olive oil
serves 4–6

PREPARATION TIME
20 minutes

COOKING TIME
25 minutes

1 For the soup: heat oil in a large heavy-based pan, add onion, potato, carrot and capsicum (pepper). Cook, uncovered, for 5 minutes over a medium heat, stirring occasionally, until vegetables begin to brown.

2 Add the stock, celery and courgettes (zucchini) and bring to the boil. Cover, reduce heat and simmer for 10 minutes or until the vegetables are tender. Stir in tomatoes and tomato purée and season generously. Simmer, uncovered, for 10 minutes.

3 For the pesto: place spring onions (green onions), parmesan and oil in a food processor and process to a fairly smooth paste. Ladle soup into bowls and top with a spoonful of pesto.

NUTRITIONAL VALUE PER SERVE	FAT **7.2** G	CARBOHYDRATE **2.9** G	PROTEIN **2.3** G

Spinach and almond soup

INGREDIENTS

450 g (14 oz) baby spinach
2¹/₂ cups (600 ml, 1 pint)
  vegetable stock
100 g (3¹/₂ oz) ground almonds
salt and black pepper
¹/₂ cup (125 ml, 4 fl oz) pouring
  cream
60 g (2 oz) parmesan, grated to
  serve

serves 4

PREPARATION TIME
5 minutes

COOKING TIME
15 minutes

1 Place spinach in a large pan with stock, reserving a few leaves for garnish. Bring to the boil, reduce heat and simmer for 5 minutes. Stir in the ground almonds and seasoning and simmer for a further 2 minutes. Remove from heat and cool a little.

2 Pour into a food processor and process until smooth. Add the cream, return to the pan and reheat gently – do not boil. Serve topped with parmesan and seasoned with black pepper. Garnish with reserved spinach leaves.

NUTRITIONAL VALUE PER SERVE   FAT **9.8** G   CARBOHYDRATE **1.2** G   PROTEIN **4.7** G

Mixed vegetable and bean soup

INGREDIENTS

2 tablespoons olive oil
1 onion, finely chopped
2 cloves garlic, crushed
1 potato, finely diced
1 carrot, finely diced
2 teaspoons cumin seeds
900 ml (1½ pints) vegetable stock
2 sticks celery, finely chopped
1 large courgette (zucchini), finely
  chopped
125 g (4 oz) fine green beans, cut into
  2.5 cm pieces
425 g (14 oz) can butter beans,
  drained
400 g (13 oz) can tomatoes, chopped
black pepper
60 g (2 oz) cheddar cheese, grated
serves 4

PREPARATION TIME
15 minutes

COOKING TIME
25 minutes

1 Heat oil in a large heavy-based pan, add onion, garlic, potato, carrot and
cumin seeds. Cook, uncovered, for 5 minutes, stirring occasionally, until
the vegetables have softened.

2 Add the stock, celery and courgette (zucchini) and bring to the boil. Cover
and simmer for 10 minutes or until the celery and courgette (zucchini)
are tender.

3 Stir in beans, butter beans, tomatoes and season to taste. Simmer,
uncovered, for 5 minutes or until the beans are tender. Pour soup into
bowls and top with cheese.

NUTRITIONAL VALUE PER SERVE	FAT **2.5** G	CARBOHYDRATE **2.5** G	PROTEIN **1.9** G

Sweet potato and rosemary soup

INGREDIENTS

3 tablespoons olive oil
2 cloves garlic, crushed
1 medium onion, chopped
1 tablespoon fresh chopped rosemary
2 tablespoons tomato pesto
1 medium carrot, diced
1 large potato, diced
750 g (1¹/₂ lb) sweet potato
1 litre (1²/₃ pints) chicken stock
freshly ground pepper and salt
extra 2 tablespoons fresh chopped
    rosemary
serves 4–6

PREPARATION TIME
20 minutes

COOKING TIME
45 minutes

1 Heat oil in a large pan, add the garlic, onion and rosemary, and cook on medium heat for 3–5 minutes, or until soft.

2 Add the tomato pesto, and cook for a further minute.

3 Add carrot, potato and sweet potato, and cook a further 5 minutes. Add the chicken stock and pepper and salt, bring to boil, reduce the heat, and simmer, covered, for 30–40 minutes, or until vegetables are soft.

4 Purée the soup in a food processor in batches, return soup to pan, add the extra rosemary, and gently heat through before serving. Add extra stock if soup is too thick.

NUTRITIONAL VALUE PER SERVE	FAT 3.9 G	CARBOHYDRATE 6.6 G	PROTEIN 1.6 G

Cream of mushroom soup with crispy onions

INGREDIENTS

2 tablespoons butter
1 tablespoon extra virgin olive oil
4 spring onions (green onions), chopped
400 g (13 oz) mushrooms, chopped
1 medium potato, peeled and chopped
900 ml (1¹/₂ pints) vegetable stock
sea salt
freshly ground black pepper
4 tablespoons thick cream
juice of ¹/₂ lemon
chopped fresh parsley
crispy onions
sunflower oil
1 large onion, finely sliced into rings
1 tablespoon plain flour
serves 4

PREPARATION TIME
15 minutes

COOKING TIME
30 minutes

1 Heat butter and oil in a large pan and fry the spring onions (green onions) and mushrooms over a medium-high heat for 5 minutes, until softened.

2 Add the potato, vegetable stock and seasoning and bring to the boil. Reduce heat, cover and simmer for 20 minutes until the potatoes are tender. Allow to cool.

3 For the onions, heat about 1 cm (¹/₂ in) oil in a large frying pan. Coat onions in the flour, add to the pan and cook for 5 minutes or until crisp and lightly golden. Drain on kitchen paper.

4 Purée the soup in a food processor and return to the pan, then stir in the cream and lemon juice and gently reheat. Ladle the soup into bowls and top with the crispy onions. Sprinkle with chopped fresh parsley, to garnish.

NUTRITIONAL VALUE PER SERVE	FAT **5.5** G	CARBOHYDRATE **2.9** G	PROTEIN **1.9** G

Minestrone soup with soda bread

INGREDIENTS

1 tablespoon vegetable oil
6 rashers rindless streaky bacon, chopped
1 onion, chopped
2 cloves garlic, chopped
1 carrot, diced
1 leek, diced
1 small potato, diced
1.2 litres (2 pints) vegetable stock
2 tablespoons tomato purée
60 g (2 oz) dried spaghetti
salt and black pepper
soda bread
250 g (8 oz) wholemeal flour
250 g (8 oz) plain flour
$^{1}/_{2}$ teaspoon salt
1 teaspoon bicarbonate of soda
4 tablespoons chilled butter, cubed
2 tablespoons chopped fresh parsley
juice of $^{1}/_{2}$ lemon
1 cup (250 ml, 8 fl oz) milk
serves 4

1 Preheat the oven to 200°C (400° F, gas mark 6). To make the bread, place the wholemeal flour into a large bowl, then sift in the plain flour, salt and bicarbonate of soda, mixing well. Rub in the butter, using fingertips, until mixture resembles coarse breadcrumbs. Mix in the parsley. Combine lemon juice and milk and stir into the flour mixture to form a soft but not sticky dough.

2 Knead the dough lightly on a floured surface and flatten slightly into a 20 cm (8 in) round. Place on a baking sheet and cut a cross into the top. Cook at the top of the oven for 35–40 minutes, until well risen and golden.

3 Heat oil in a large pan. Add the bacon, onion, garlic, carrot, leek and potato and cook for 5–10 minutes or until softened. Pour in the stock and tomato purée, then simmer, covered, for 20 minutes or until vegetables are tender. Break the spaghetti into 2.5 cm (1 in) lengths and add to the pan. Cook for 10 minutes or until the pasta is al dente. Season to taste and serve with the bread.

PREPARATION TIME
30 minutes

COOKING TIME
40 minutes

NUTRITIONAL VALUE PER SERVE	FAT **11.5** G	CARBOHYDRATE **14.9** G	PROTEIN **5.2** G

Creamy oyster bisque

INGREDIENTS

20 fresh oysters, shucked
low-salt fish or vegetable stock
$^1/_2$ cup (125 ml, 4 fl oz) white wine
1 small white onion, diced
1 stalk celery, diced
400 g (13 oz) potato, peeled and
  diced
1 tablespoon chopped fresh thyme
$^1/_2$ cup (125 ml, 4 fl oz) low-fat milk
freshly ground black pepper
sprigs watercress or fresh parsley,
  optional

serves 4

PREPARATION TIME
20 minutes

COOKING TIME
25 minutes

1 Pour any liquid from the oysters into a cup. Add enough stock to make up to 1 cup (250 ml, 8 fl oz).

2 Heat 2 tablespoons of the wine in a large pan over a low heat. Add onion and celery. Cook, stirring, for 4–5 minutes or until onion is transparent. Add potato and thyme. Stir in stock mixture and remaining wine. Bring to the boil. Reduce heat and simmer for 10–15 minutes or until potatoes are tender and most of the liquid is absorbed. Cool slightly.

3 Transfer mixture to a food processor or blender. Add half the oysters, the milk and black pepper to taste. Purée. Return mixture to a clean pan. Bring to the boil. Remove soup from heat. Stir in remaining oysters.

4 To serve, ladle soup into warm bowls and top with watercress sprigs or parsley, if desired.

NUTRITIONAL VALUE PER SERVE	FAT 0.7 G	CARBOHYDRATE 5.4 G	PROTEIN 4.4 G

Hot-and-sour scallop soup

INGREDIENTS

1 litre (1²/₃ pints) chicken stock
125 g (4 oz) mushrooms, thinly sliced
60 g (2 oz) bamboo shoots, sliced
250 g (8 oz) sea or bay scallops, sliced
   5 mm (¹/₄ in) thick
1 teaspoon soy sauce
¹/₄ teaspoon white pepper
2 tablespoons cornflour
3 tablespoons warm water
1 egg, beaten
3 tablespoons rice vinegar
2 spring onions (green onions),
   thinly sliced
serves 4

PREPARATION TIME
20 minutes

COOKING TIME
25 minutes

1   Place chicken stock, mushrooms and bamboo shoots in a large
    pan. Bring to the boil, reduce heat and simmer 5 minutes. Rinse
    scallops under cold running water. Add scallops, soy sauce and
    pepper to the pan. Bring to the boil.

2   Combine cornflour and warm water. Add to the soup and stir
    until thickened. Stir briskly with a chopstick while gradually
    pouring in egg. Remove from heat. Stir in rice vinegar (white-wine
    vinegar may be substituted); sprinkle with spring onions (green
    onions). Serve immediately.

NUTRITIONAL VALUE PER SERVE   FAT **0.8** G   CARBOHYDRATE **2.6** G   PROTEIN **3.4** G

Tricolore canapés

INGREDIENTS

cucumber bowls
1 cucumber
100 g (3½ oz) cream cheese
1 tablespoon chopped fresh
   tarragon
salt and black pepper

tomato toasts
3 slices thick-cut sandwich loaf
1 clove garlic, crushed
3 tablespoons olive oil
2 tablespoons pesto
150 g (9 oz) mozzarella cheese, cut
   into 12 slices
3 small tomatoes, thinly sliced
   and ends discarded
12 small pitted black olives

salmon rounds
4 slices dark or light rye bread
1 tablespoon butter, softened
150 g (5 oz) smoked salmon, cut
   into ribbons
2 teaspoons lemon juice
3 tablespoons fromage frais
1 teaspoon horseradish cream

serves 6

1 Refrigerate sandwich and rye breads for 2 hours.

2 Make the cucumber bowls: peel strips of skin from the length of the cucumber to give a striped effect and cut into 1 cm (½ in) thick rounds. Using a teaspoon, remove some seeds from each round to make a hollow. Pat dry. In a small bowl, combine cream cheese, tarragon, salt and pepper. Fill cucumber hollows with cream cheese mixture, season with black pepper and refrigerate for 1 hour.

3 For the tomato toasts: preheat oven to 200°C (400°F, gas mark 6). Using a 5 cm (2 in) pastry cutter, cut out 4 rounds from each slice of the chilled sandwich bread. Combine garlic and oil. Brush a baking tray with half the garlic oil, place the rounds on baking tray and brush with remaining oil. Cook for 10 minutes or until golden. Cool, and spread with pesto and top with mozzarella, tomatoes and olives. Season with pepper and serve.

4 For the salmon rounds: cut out 3 rounds from each slice of chilled rye bread with a 5 cm (2 in) pastry cutter and brush with softened butter. Combine salmon, lemon juice, fromage frais, horseradish and seasoning in a small bowl. Spoon a small amount onto each round and serve.

PREPARATION TIME
15 minutes, plus
2 hours refrigeration

COOKING TIME
6 minutes

NUTRITIONAL VALUE PER SERVE	FAT 12.2 G	CARBOHYDRATE 10 G	PROTEIN 8 G

Tzatziki

INGREDIENTS

³/₄ cup (185 g, 6 oz) plain
  Greek yoghurt
90 g (3 oz) grated cucumber
1 tablespoon lemon juice
1 clove garlic, crushed
salt and black pepper
1 tablespoon chopped
  fresh mint

**makes 1 cup
  (250 ml, 8 fl oz)**

1 In a large bowl, combine all ingredients, and season with salt and pepper to taste. Cover and refrigerate for at least 1 hour (to allow the flavours to develop).

2 Serve with pita bread as a dip, or as an accompaniment sauce.

PREPARATION TIME
15 minutes

NUTRITIONAL VALUE PER SERVE	FAT **4.3** G	CARBOHYDRATE **6.5** G	PROTEIN **3.7** G

Roasted aubergine and garlic dip

INGREDIENTS

1 large aubergine (eggplant)
5 cloves garlic, roasted
1 tablespoon olive oil
1 tablespoon tahini (sesame paste)
1 tablespoon lemon juice
1 tablespoon olive oil
salt and black pepper
makes 2 cups (500 ml, 16 fl oz)

1 Preheat the oven to 200°C (400°F, gas mark 6).

2 Place the eggplant and garlic on a baking tray, drizzle with olive oil and roast in the oven for 20 minutes. Remove from oven, scoop out flesh from eggplant and place the flesh and roasted garlic in a food processor.

3 Process until smooth, add tahini, lemon juice and olive oil, and process for a further few seconds to combine.

4 Season to taste and serve with bread.

PREPARATION TIME
**15 minutes, plus
30 minutes
refrigeration**
COOKING TIME
20 minutes

NUTRITIONAL VALUE PER SERVE	FAT **9.9** G	CARBOHYDRATE **3** G	PROTEIN **2.7** G

Breadsticks wrapped in parma ham and rocket

INGREDIENTS

15 g (½ oz) rocket
3 tablespoons olive oil
6 thin slices parma
  ham
6 breadsticks
makes 6

1 Brush rocket or basil leaves with a little oil. Place a few leaves in the middle of each ham slice, then place a breadstick in the centre, leaving about 7.5 cm (3 in) uncovered to use as a handle.

2 Tightly wrap the ham around the breadstick, tucking it in neatly at the top. Brush ham with the remaining oil. Serve.

PREPARATION TIME
5 minutes

NUTRITIONAL VALUE PER SERVE   FAT **25.4** G   CARBOHYDRATE **16.4** G   PROTEIN **1.8** G

Apricots with walnuts and bacon

INGREDIENTS

2 slices rindless bacon
12 walnut halves
6 dried apricots
serves 6

1 Preheat grill to high. Stretch each bacon rasher with the back of a knife, then cut into 3 pieces. Place 2 walnut halves inside each apricot and wrap a piece of bacon around it. Secure with a moistened tooth pick.

2 Grill the wrapped apricots for 2 minutes each side until crisp and golden. Serve immediately.

PREPARATION TIME
5 minutes

COOKING TIME
5 minutes

NUTRITIONAL VALUE PER SERVE   FAT **20.5** G   CARBOHYDRATE **7.6** G   PROTEIN **16.7** G

Scallop and watercress salad

INGREDIENTS

10 fresh scallops

90 g (3 oz) watercress; discard
   woody stems, select tender tips
   only

160 g (5^1/$_2$ oz) water chestnuts,
   halved

4 cherry tomatoes

50 g (1^3/$_4$ oz) walnut halves

90 g (3 oz) bean shoots

dressing

^{2}/$_3$ cup (170 ml, 5^1/$_2$ fl oz) walnut or
   olive oil

2 tablespoons red-wine vinegar

2 small cloves garlic, crushed

salt and white pepper

serves 4

1 Combine dressing ingredients in a jar and shake well.

2 Place the scallops on a plate suitable for steaming. Sprinkle scallops with a little of the dressing and steam gently over boiling water for 6 minutes.

3 Snap watercress into 10 cm (4 in) sections. In a large serving bowl, combine watercress, water chestnuts, cherry tomatoes, walnuts and bean shoots. Pour over the dressing and toss gently to coat well. Gently mix in the scallops and serve.

PREPARATION TIME
10 minutes
COOKING TIME
6 minutes

NUTRITIONAL VALUE PER SERVE	FAT **24.2** G	CARBOHYDRATE **2.8** G	PROTEIN **3.7** G

Anchovy, egg and parmesan salad

INGREDIENTS

3 medium eggs
2 heads endive (chicory)
2 small butter lettuces, leaves torn
12 anchovy fillets in oil, drained and
   cut in half lengthways
1 tablespoon capers, drained
3 cherry tomatoes, halved
50 g ($1^3/_4$ oz) parmesan cheese
3 tablespoons extra virgin olive oil
juice of 1 lemon
salt and black pepper
fresh flat-leaf parsley to garnish
serves 6

1 Bring a small pan of water to the boil, add eggs and boil for 10 minutes. Remove from pan, cool under cold running water, then shell. Cut each egg lengthways into quarters.

2 On each serving plate, arrange 8 alternating endive and lettuce leaves, tips facing outwards, in a star shape. Place 2 egg quarters on the base of 2 opposite lettuce leaves, then place 2 anchovy halves on the other 2 opposite lettuce leaves. Scatter the capers over the leaves.

3 Put a cherry tomato half in the centre of each plate and drape 2 anchovy halves over the top. Shave over the parmesan, using a vegetable peeler, then drizzle over the olive oil and lemon juice. Season to taste and garnish with parsley.

PREPARATION TIME
10 minutes

COOKING TIME
10 minutes

NUTRITIONAL VALUE PER SERVE	FAT 5.0 G	CARBOHYDRATE 0.6 G	PROTEIN 3.7 G

Tomato toasts with fresh basil

INGREDIENTS

4 tablespoons olive oil
½ teaspoon mixed dried herbs
black pepper
1 long bread stick (baguette), cut
  into 12 slices
8 plum tomatoes
1 clove garlic, crushed
30 g (1 oz) sun-dried tomatoes in oil,
  drained and finely chopped
1 teaspoon vinegar
1 teaspoon sugar
2 tablespoons chopped fresh basil
serves 4

PREPARATION TIME
10 minutes

COOKING TIME
15 minutes

1 Preheat oven to 220°C (425°F, gas mark 7). Combine 3 tablespoons of the oil with the dried herbs and season well. Brush both sides of each bread slice with the flavoured oil. Cook for 8 minutes or until lightly golden and crisp.

2 In a large bowl, place tomatoes and cover with boiling water. Leave for 30 seconds. Peel and deseed, then roughly chop the flesh. Set aside.

3 Heat the remaining olive oil in a large frying pan, add garlic, chopped tomatoes, sun-dried tomatoes, vinegar, sugar and basil. Cook, stirring occasionally, for 5 minutes or until heated through. Remove from heat. Spoon tomato mixture onto each of toasts, season and serve.

NUTRITIONAL VALUE PER SERVE	FAT **8.6** G	CARBOHYDRATE **25.2** G	PROTEIN **4.7** G

Thai fish cakes

INGREDIENTS

500 g (1 lb) boneless firm white
fish fillets, skinned
3 spring onions (green onions),
chopped
1 egg, lightly beaten
2 tablespoons plain flour
2 fresh red chillies, deseeded and
chopped
$1/2$ teaspoon cumin seeds
2 teaspoons grated fresh ginger
vegetable oil for shallow-frying
coriander chutney
1 bunch fresh coriander (cilantro)
4 spring onions (green onions),
chopped
1 tablespoon grated fresh ginger
1 clove garlic, crushed
2 tablespoons lime or lemon juice
1 tablespoon vegetable oil
serves 4–6

PREPARATION TIME
25 minutes

COOKING TIME
10 minutes

1 Place fish in a food processor and process until finely chopped. Add spring onions
(green onions), egg, flour, chillies, cumin seeds and ginger and process to make a
stiff paste.

2 Take 2 tablespoons of fish mixture and shape into a small flat cake. Place on a
plate lined with plastic food wrap. Repeat with remaining mixture.

3 Heat oil in a frying pan over a medium heat and cook fish cakes in batches for
3–4 minutes each side or until cooked. Set aside and keep warm.

4 For the chutney: place coriander (cilantro), spring onions (green onions), ginger,
garlic, lime or lemon juice and oil in a food processor and process until smooth.
Serve with warm fish cakes.

NUTRITIONAL VALUE PER SERVE	FAT **14.7** G	CARBOHYDRATE **2.5** G	PROTEIN **11.3** G

Nut-crusted fish bites

INGREDIENTS

50 g (1³/₄ oz) hazelnuts, chopped
60 g (2 oz) fresh breadcrumbs
30 g (1 oz) plain flour
salt and black pepper
1 large egg, beaten
vegetable oil for shallow-frying
500 g (1 lb) firm white fish fillet, cut
  into 20 even-sized pieces
tartare sauce, vinegar or lemon juice
  to serve

serves 4

1 In a large shallow bowl, combine the nuts and breadcrumbs. Place flour into another bowl and season. Place egg into a third bowl. Dip the fish pieces into flour, then egg and finally the breadcrumb mixture to coat. Set aside.

2 Heat 1 cm (¹/₂ in) of oil in a large frying pan and fry fish pieces in batches for 5 minutes or until golden on all sides. Drain on kitchen towels and keep warm. Serve with tartare sauce or sprinkled with vinegar or lemon juice.

PREPARATION TIME
15 minutes

COOKING TIME
15 minutes

NUTRITIONAL VALUE PER SERVE   FAT **20.2** G   CARBOHYDRATE **8.1** G   PROTEIN **15.7** G

Potato cakes with smoked salmon

INGREDIENTS

300 g (10 oz) floury potatoes, unpeeled
150 ml (5 fl oz) milk
salt and black pepper
1 large egg
30 g (1 oz) plain flour
4 spring onions (green onions), finely
 sliced
1 tablespoon oil
$^1/_2$ cup (125 ml, 4 fl oz) crème fraîche
2 tablespoons chopped fresh dill
150 g (5 oz) smoked salmon slices
freshly ground black pepper
extra dill to garnish
lemon wedges to serve
serves 4

1 Cook the potatoes in boiling salted water for 15–20 minutes until tender, then drain. Cool for a few minutes, then peel. Mash with milk, season, then beat in the egg, flour and spring onions (green onions) to make a batter.

2 Heat a large non-stick frying pan, add a little of the oil. Make 4 potato cakes, using 2 tablespoons of batter for each. Fry for 2–3 minutes on each side until golden. Drain on kitchen towels and keep warm while you make 2 further batches of 4 potato cakes.

3 Combine the crème fraîche and chopped dill. Serve pancakes topped with the salmon slices and a spoonful of crème fraîche mixture. Garnish with black pepper, dill and serve with lemon wedges.

PREPARATION TIME
15 minutes

COOKING TIME
40 minutes

| NUTRITIONAL VALUE PER SERVE | FAT 7.9 G | CARBOHYDRATE 8.5 G | PROTEIN 6.9 G |

Glossary

Al dente: Italian term to describe pasta and rice that are cooked until tender but still firm to the bite.

Bake blind: to bake pastry cases without their fillings. Line the raw pastry case with greaseproof paper and fill with raw rice or dried beans to prevent collapsed sides and puffed base. Remove paper and fill 5 minutes before completion of cooking time.

Baste: to spoon hot cooking liquid over food at intervals during cooking to moisten and flavour it.

Beat: to make a mixture smooth with rapid and regular motions using a spatula, wire whisk or electric mixer; to make a mixture light and smooth by enclosing air.

Beurre manié: equal quantities of butter and flour mixed together to a smooth paste and stirred bit by bit into a soup, stew or sauce while on the heat to thicken. Stop adding when desired thickness results.

Bind: to add egg or a thick sauce to hold ingredients together when cooked.

Blanch: to plunge some foods into boiling water for less than a minute and immediately plunge into iced water. This is to brighten the colour of some vegetables and to remove skin from tomatoes and nuts.

Blend: to mix 2 or more ingredients thoroughly together; do not confuse with blending in an electric blender.

Boil: to cook in a liquid brought to boiling point and kept there.

Boiling point: when bubbles rise continually and break over the entire surface of the liquid, reaching a temperature of 100°C (212°F). In some cases food is held at this high temperature for a few seconds then heat is turned to low for slower cooking. See *simmer*.

Bouquet garni: a bundle of several herbs tied together with string for easy removal, placed into pots of stock, soups and stews for flavour. A few sprigs of fresh thyme, parsley and bay leaf are used. Can be purchased in sachet form for convenience.

Caramelise: to heat sugar in a heavy-based pan until it liquefies and develops a caramel colour. Vegetables such as blanched carrots and sautéed onions may be sprinkled with sugar and caramelised.

Chill: to place in the refrigerator or stir over ice until cold.

Clarify: to make a liquid clear by removing sediments and impurities. To melt fat and remove any sediment.

Coat: to dust or roll food items in flour to cover the surface before the food is cooked. Also, to coat in flour, egg and breadcrumbs.

Cool: to stand at room temperature until some or all heat is removed, eg cool a little, cool completely.

Cream: to make creamy and fluffy by working the mixture with the back of a wooden spoon; usually refers to creaming butter and sugar or margarine. May also be done with an electric mixer.

Croutons: small cubes of bread, toasted or fried, used as an addition to salads or as a garnish to soups and stews.

Crudités: raw vegetable sticks served with a dipping sauce.

Crumb: to coat foods in flour, egg and breadcrumbs to form a protective coating for foods which are fried. Also adds flavour and texture and enhances appearance.

Cube: to cut into small pieces with six even sides, eg cubes of meat.

Cut in: to combine fat, such as butter or shortening, and flour using 2 knives scissor-fashion or a pastry blender, to make pastry.

Deglaze: to dissolve dried-out cooking juices left on the base and sides of a roasting dish or frying pan. Add a little water, wine or stock, scrape and stir over heat until dissolved. Resulting liquid is used to make a flavoursome gravy or added to a sauce or casserole.

Degrease: to skim fat from the surface of cooking liquids, eg stocks, soups, casseroles.

Dice: to cut into small cubes.

Dredge: to heavily coat with icing sugar, sugar, flour or cornflour.

Dressing: a mixture added to completed dishes to add moisture and flavour, eg salads, cooked vegetables.

Drizzle: to pour in a fine thread-like stream moving over a surface.

Egg wash: beaten egg with milk or water used to brush over pastry, bread dough or biscuits to give a sheen and golden brown colour.

Essence: a strong flavouring liquid, usually made by distillation. Only a few drops are needed to flavour.

Fillet: a piece of prime meat, fish or poultry which is boneless or has all bones removed.

Flake: to separate cooked fish into flakes, removing any bones and skin, using 2 forks.

Flame: to ignite warmed alcohol over food or to pour into a pan with food, ignite, then serve.

Flute: to make decorative indentations around the pastry rim before baking.

Fold in: combining of a light, whisked or creamed mixture with other ingredients. Add a portion of the other ingredients at a time and mix using a gentle circular motion, over and under the mixture so that air will not be lost. Use a metal spoon or spatula.

Glaze: to brush or coat food with a liquid that will give the finished product a glossy appearance, and on baked products, a golden brown colour.

Grease: to rub the surface of a metal or heatproof dish with oil or fat, to prevent the food from sticking.

Herbed butter: softened butter mixed with finely chopped fresh herbs and re-chilled. Used to serve on grilled meats and fish.

Hors d'oeuvre: small savoury foods served as an appetiser, popularly known today as 'finger food'.

Infuse: to steep foods in a liquid until the liquid absorbs their flavour.

Joint: to cut poultry and game into serving pieces by dividing at the joint.

Julienne: to cut some food, eg vegetables and processed meats, into fine strips the length of matchsticks. Used in salads or as a garnish to cooked dishes.

Knead: to work a yeast dough in a pressing, stretching and folding motion with the heel of the hand until smooth and elastic to develop the gluten strands. Non-yeast doughs should be lightly and quickly handled as gluten development is not desired.

Line: to cover the inside of a baking tin with paper for the easy removal of the cooked product from the baking tin.

Macerate: to stand fruit in a syrup, liqueur or spirit to give added flavour.

Marinade: a flavoured liquid, into which food is placed for some time to give it flavour and to tenderise. Marinades include an acid ingredient such as vinegar or wine, oil and seasonings.

Mask: to evenly cover cooked food portions with a sauce, mayonnaise or savoury jelly.

Pan-fry: to fry foods in a small amount of fat or oil, sufficient to coat the base of the pan.

Parboil: to boil until partially cooked. The food is then finished by some other method.

Pare: to peel the skin from vegetables and fruit. 'Peel' is the popular term but 'pare' is the name given to the knife used; paring knife.

Pit: to remove stones or seeds from olives, cherries, dates.

Pith: the white lining between the rind and flesh of oranges, grapefruit and lemons.

Pitted: the olives, cherries, dates etc. with the stone removed, eg purchase pitted dates.

Poach: to simmer gently in enough hot liquid to almost cover the food so its shape will be retained.

Pound: to flatten meats with a meat mallet; to reduce to a paste or small particles with a mortar and pestle.

Simmer: to cook in liquid just below boiling point at about 96°C (205°F) with small bubbles rising gently to the surface.

Skim: to remove fat or froth from the surface of simmering food.

Stock: the liquid produced when meat, poultry, fish or vegetables have been simmered in water to extract the flavour. Used as a base for soups, sauces, casseroles etc. Convenience stock products are available.

Sweat: to cook sliced onions or vegetables in a small amount of butter in a covered pan over low heat, to soften them and release flavour without colouring.

Conversions

Measurements differ from country to country, so it's important to understand what the differences are. This Measurements Guide gives you simple 'at-a-glance' information for using the recipes in this book, wherever you may be.

Cooking is not an exact science – minor variations in measurements won't make a difference to your cooking.

EQUIPMENT
There is a difference in the size of measuring cups used internationally, but the difference is minimal (only 2–3 teaspoons). We use the Australian standard metric measurements in our recipes:

1 teaspoon.....5 ml	1 tablespoon.....20 ml
1/2 cup.....125 ml	1 cup.....250 ml
4 cups.....1 litre	

Measuring cups come in sets of one cup (250 ml), 1/2 cup (125 ml), 1/3 cup (80 ml) and 1/4 cup (60 ml). Use these for measuring liquids and certain dry ingredients.

Measuring spoons come in a set of four and should be used for measuring dry and liquid ingredients.

When using cup or spoon measures, always make them level (unless the recipe indicates otherwise).

DRY VERSUS WET INGREDIENTS
While this system of measures is consistent for liquids, it's more difficult to quantify dry ingredients. For instance, one level cup equals: 200 g of brown sugar; 210 g of caster sugar; and 110 g of icing sugar.

When measuring dry ingredients such as flour, don't push the flour down or shake it into the cup. It is best just to spoon the flour in until it reaches the desired amount. When measuring liquids, use a clear vessel indicating metric levels.

Always use medium eggs (55–60 g) when eggs are required in a recipe.

OVEN
Your oven should always be at the right temperature before placing the food in it to be cooked. Note that if your oven doesn't have a fan you may need to cook food for a little longer.

MICROWAVE
It is difficult to give an exact cooking time for microwave cooking. It is best to watch what you are cooking closely to monitor its progress.

STANDING TIME
Many foods continue to cook when you take them out of the oven or microwave. If a recipe states that the food needs to 'stand' after cooking, be sure not to overcook the dish.

CAN SIZES
The can sizes available in your supermarket or grocery store may not be the same as specified in the recipe. Don't worry if there is a small variation in size – it's unlikely to make a difference to the end result.

dry		liquids	
metric (grams)	imperial (ounces)	metric (millilitres)	imperial (fluid ounces)
		30 ml	1 fl oz
30 g	1 oz	60 ml	2 fl oz
60 g	2 oz	90 ml	3 fl oz
90 g	3 oz	100 ml	3 1/2 fl oz
100 g	3 1/2 oz	125 ml	4 fl oz
125 g	4 oz	150 ml	5 fl oz
150 g	5 oz	190 ml	6 fl oz
185 g	6 oz	250 ml	8 fl oz
200 g	7 oz	300 ml	10 fl oz
250 g	8 oz	500 ml	16 fl oz
280 g	9 oz	600 ml	20 fl oz (1 pint)*
315 g	10 oz	1000 ml (1 litre)	32 fl oz
330 g	11 oz		
370 g	12 oz		
400 g	13 oz		
440 g	14 oz		
470 g	15 oz		
500 g	16 oz (1 lb)		
750 g	24 oz (1 1/2 lb)		
1000 g (1 kg)	32 oz (2 lb)	*Note: an American pint is 16 fl oz.	

cooking temperatures	°C (celsius)	°F (fahrenheit)	gas mark
very slow	120	250	1/2
slow	150	300	2
moderately slow	160	315	2–3
moderate	180	350	4
moderately hot	190	375	5
	200	400	6
hot	220	425	7
very hot	230	450	8
	240	475	9
	250	500	10

Index

Essential COOKING SERIES

COMPREHENSIVE, STEP-BY-STEP COOKING

Essential COOKING SERIES
COMPREHENSIVE, STEP-BY-STEP COOKING
Baking

Essential COOKING SERIES
COMPREHENSIVE, STEP-BY-STEP COOKING
Chicken Meals

Essential COOKING SERIES
COMPREHENSIVE, STEP-BY-STEP COOKING
Salads & Greens

Essential COOKING SERIES
COMPREHENSIVE, STEP-BY-STEP COOKING
Soups & Hors D'Oeuvres

Essential COOKING SERIES
COMPREHENSIVE, STEP-BY-STEP COOKING
Meat Dishes

Essential COOKING SERIES
COMPREHENSIVE, STEP-BY-STEP COOKING
Finger Food

Essential COOKING SERIES
COMPREHENSIVE, STEP-BY-STEP COOKING
Pasta Dishes

Essential COOKING SERIES
COMPREHENSIVE, STEP-BY-STEP COOKING
Grilling & Barbecuing
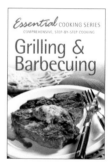

Essential COOKING SERIES
COMPREHENSIVE, STEP-BY-STEP COOKING
Rice & Risotto

Essential COOKING SERIES
Comprehensive, Step-by-step cooking
Vegetarian Dishes
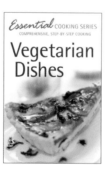

Essential COOKING SERIES
COMPREHENSIVE, STEP-BY-STEP COOKING
Asian Dishes
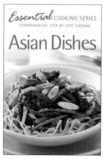

Essential COOKING SERIES
COMPREHENSIVE, STEP-BY-STEP COOKING
Stir-Fry